I0007838

Python for Data Science

How to learn basic contents to work with data with this programming language with this beginner's guide. Machine learning tools, concepts, and data analysis crash course.

Matthew Arduino

Legal & Disclaimer

The information contained in this book and its contents is not designed to replace or take the place of any form of medical or professional advice; and is not meant to replace the need for independent medical, financial, legal or other professional advice or services, as may be required. The content and information in this book has been provided for educational and entertainment purposes only.

The content and information contained in this book has been compiled from sources deemed reliable, and it is accurate to the best of the Author's knowledge, information and belief. However, the Author cannot guarantee its accuracy and validity and cannot be held liable for any errors and/or omissions. Further, changes are periodically made to this book as and when needed.

Where appropriate and/or necessary, you must consult a professional (including but not limited to your doctor, attorney, financial advisor or such other professional advisor) before using any of the suggested remedies, techniques, or information in this book.

Upon using the contents and information contained in this book, you agree to hold harmless the Author from and against any damages, costs, and expenses, including any legal fees potentially resulting from the application of any of the information provided by this book. This disclaimer applies to any loss, damages or injury caused by the use and application, whether directly or indirectly, of any advice or information presented, whether for breach of contract, tort, negligence, personal injury, criminal intent, or under any other cause of action.

You agree to accept all risks of using the information presented inside this book.

You agree that by continuing to read this book, where appropriate and/or necessary, you shall consult a professional (including but not limited to your doctor, attorney, or financial advisor or such other advisor as needed) before using any of the suggested remedies, techniques, or information in this book.

Table of Contents

INTRODUCTION

Python is one of today's most powerful and beginner friendly programming languages. In recent years it has gained more ground as the technology of choice for fields such as Machine Learning, Deep Learning, and Data Science. There's never been a better time to start learning how to program with Python.

The purpose of this book is to make this amazing programming language as available as possible, no matter your current skill and knowledge of programming. With the help of this guide you will get started in no time, even if your knowledge on the topic is nonexistent.

Every chapter in this book is layered in such a way to teach you every core programming concept step by step. Furthermore, you will not learn only theory and challenging definitions that make you fall asleep. You will go through a number of practical examples and exercises in parallel and practice everything you learn. Keep in mind that without practicing every concept and writing your own code you will not manage to get too far. Programming doesn't require any special talents. All you need is practice, practice, and more practice. So let this book guide you, and make sure you take a break every now and then to experiment and come up with your own little programs. Python is the future!

Chapter 1: Fundamentals of Python for Data Science

History of data science

The history of deep learning can be traced back to 1943, when Warren McCulloch and Walter Pitts published a paper with a concept of Artificial Neuron(AN) to mimic the thought process. This Artificial neuron was based on the characteristic of a biological neuron of either being fully active to a stimulation or none at all. This behavior of biological neurons was observed in microelectrode readings from brain. In 1957, Frank and Rosenblatt

presented Mark I Perceptron Machine as the first implementation of the perceptron algorithm. The idea was to resemble the working of biological neurons to create an agent that can learn. This perceptron was a supervised binary linear classifier with adjustable weights. This functionality was implemented through following function: Where, w is weights vector, X is inputs and b is bias. For each input and output pair, this formula provided classification results. If the result/

prediction did not match with output, the weight vector was updated through : Where, is predicted/ output of function, is actual output, is input vector and is weight vector.

It should be noted that back at that time, they implemented this functionality through a hardware machine with wires and connections (as shown in the figure below).

In 1960, Widrow and Hoff stacked these perceptrons and built a 3-layered (input layer, hidden layer, output layer), fully connected, feed-forward architecture for classification as a hardware implementation, called ADALINE. The architecture presented in the paper is shown in image below.

In 1960, Henry J. Kelley introduced a continuous back propagation model, which is currently used in learning weights of the model. In 1962, a simpler version of backpropagation based on chain rule was introduced by Stuart Dreyfus but these methods were inefficient. The backpropagation currently used in models was actually presented in 1980s. In 1979, Fukushima designed a multi-layered convolutional neural network architecture, called Neocognitron, that could learn to recognize patterns in images. The network resembled to current day architectures but wasn't exactly the same. It also allowed to manually adjust the weight of certain connections. Many concepts from Neocognitron continue to be used. The layered connections in perceptrons allowed to develop a variety of neural networks. For several patterns present in the data, Selective Attention Model could distinguish and separate them. In 1970, Seppo Linnainmaa presented automatic differentiation to efficiently compute the derivative of a differentiable composite function using chain rule. Its application, later in 1986, led to the backpropagation of errors in multilayer perceptrons. This was when Geoff Hinton, Williams and Rumelhart presented a paper to demonstrate that backpropagation in neural networks provides interesting distribution representations. In 1989, Yann LeCun, currently, Director of AI Research Facebook, provided first practical demonstration of backpropagation in convolutional neural networks to read handwritten digits at Bell Labs. Even though with backpropagation, deep neural networks were not being able to train well. In 1995, Vapnik and Cortes introduced support vector machines for regression and classification of data. In 1997, Schmidhuber and Hochreiter introduced Long Short Term Memory (LSTM) for recurrent neural networks. In all these years, a major hindering constraint was computed but in 1999, computers started to become faster at processing data and Graphical Processing Units (GPUs) were introduced. This immensely increased the compute power. In 2006, Hinton and Salakhutdinov presented a paper that reinvigorated research in deep learning. This was the first time when a proper 10 layer convolutional neural network was trained properly. Instead of training 10 layers using backpropagation, they came up with an unsupervised pre-training scheme, called Restricted Boltzmann Machine. This was a 2 step approach for training. In the first step, each layer of the network was trained using unsupervised objective. In the second step, all the layers were stacked together for backpropagation.

Later in 2009, Fei-Fei Li, a professor at Stanford university launched ImageNet, a large visual database designed for visual object recognition research containing more than 14 million hand-annotated images of 20,000 different object categories. This gave neural networks a huge edge as data of this order made it possible to train neural networks and achieve good results.

In 2010, neural networks got a lot of attention from the research community when Microsoft presented a paper on speech recognition and neural networks performed really well compared to other machine learning tools like SVMs and kernels. Specifically, they introduced neural network as a part of GMM and HMM framework and achieved huge improvements.

In 2012, a paper by Krizhevsky, Sutskever and Hinton showed that huge improvements are achieved through deep learning in the visual recognition domain.

Their model, AlexNet outperformed all the other traditional computer vision methods in visual recognition task and won several international competitions. Since then, the field has exploded and several network architectures and ideas have been introduced like GANs.

How to install python

Since many aspiring data scientists never used Python before, we're going to discuss the installation process to familiarize you with various packages and distributions that you will need later.

Before we begin, it's worth taking note that there are two versions of Python, namely Python 2 and Python 3. You can use either of them however Python 3 is the future. Many data scientists still use Python 2, but the shift to version 3 has been building up gradually. What's important to keep in mind is that there are various compatibility issues between the two versions. This means that if you write a program using Python 2 and then run it inside a Python 3 interpreter, the code might not work. The developers behind Python have also stopped focusing on Python 2, therefore version 3 is the one that is being constantly developed and improved. With that being said, let's go through the step by step installation process.

Step by Step Setup

Start by going to Python's webpage at www.python.org and download Python. Next, we will go through the manual installation which requires several steps and instructions. It is not obligatory to setup Python manually, however, this gives you great control over the installation and it's important for future installations that you will perform independently depending on each of your projects' specifications. The easier way of installing Python is through automatically installing a scientific data distribution, which sets you up with all the packages and tools you may need (including a lot that you won't need). Therefore, if you wish to go through the simplified installation method, head down to the section about scientific distributions.

When you download Python from the developer's website, make sure to choose the correct installer depending on your machine's operating system. Afterwards, simply run the installer. Python is now installed, however, it is not quite ready for our purposes. We will now have to install various packages. The easiest way to do this is to open the command console and type "pip" to bring up the package manager. The "easy_install" package manager is an alternative, but pip is widely considered an improvement. If you run the commands and nothing happens, it means that you need to download and install any of these managers. Just head to their respective websites and go through a basic installation process to get them. But why bother with a package manager as a beginner?

A package manager like "pip" will make it a lot easier for you to install / uninstall packages, or roll them back if the package version causes some incompatibility issues or errors. Because of this advantage of streamlining the process, most new Python installations come with pip pre-installed. Now let's learn how to install a package. If you chose "pip", simply type the following line in the command console:

pip install < package_name >

If you chose "Easy Install", the process remains the same. Just type:

easy_install < package_name >

Once the command is given, the specified package will be downloaded and installed together with any other dependencies they require in order to run. We will go over the most important packages that you will require in a later section. For now, it's enough to understand the basic setup process.

Scientific Distributions

As you can see in the previous section, building your working environment can be somewhat time consuming. After installing Python, you need to choose the packages you need for your project and install them one at a time. Installing many different packages and tools can lead to failed installations and errors. This can often result in a massive loss of time for an aspiring data scientist who doesn't fully understand the subtleties behind certain errors. Finding solutions to them isn't always straightforward. This is why you have the option of directly downloading and installing a scientific distribution.

Automatically building and setting up your environment can save you from spending time and frustration on installations and allow you to jump straight in. A scientific distribution usually contains all the libraries you need, an Integrated Development Environment (IDE), and various tools. Let's discuss the most popular distributions and their application.

Anaconda

This is probably the most complete scientific distribution offered by Continuum Analytics. It comes with close to 200 packages pre-installed, including Matplotlib, Scikit-learn, NumPy, pandas, and more (we'll discuss these packages a bit later). Anaconda can be used on any machine, no matter the operating system, and can be installed next to any other distributions. The purpose is to offer the user everything they need for analytics, scientific computing, and mass-processing. It's also worth mentioning that it comes with its own package manager pre-installed, ready for you to use in order to manage packages. This is a powerful distribution, and luckily it can be downloaded and installed for free, however there is an advanced version that requires purchase.

If you use Anaconda, you will be able to access "conda" in order to install, update, or remove various packages. This package manager can also be used to install virtual environments (more on that later). For now, let's focus on the commands. First, you need to make sure you are running the latest version of conda. You can check and update by typing the following command in the command line:

conda update conda

Now, let's say you know which package you want to install. Type the following command:

conda install < package_name >

If you want to install multiple packages, you can list them one after another in the same command line. Here's an example:

conda install < package_number_1 > < package_number_2 > < package_number_3 >

Next, you might need to update some existing packages. This can be done with the following command:

conda update < package_name >

You also have the ability to update all the packages at once. Simply type:

conda update --all

The last basic command you should be aware of for now is the one for package removal. Type the following command to uninstall a certain package:

conda remove < package_name >

This tool is similar to "pip" and "easy install", and even though it's usually included with Anaconda, it can also be installed separately because it works with other scientific distributions as well.

Canopy

This is another scientific distribution popular because it's aimed towards data scientists and analysts. It also comes with around 200 pre-installed packages and includes the most popular ones you will use later, such as Matplotlib and pandas. If you choose to use this distribution instead of Anaconda, type the following command to install it:

canopy_cli

Keep in mind that you will only have access to the basic version of Canopy without paying. If you will ever require its advanced features, you will have to download and install the full version.

WinPython

If you are running on a Windows operating system, you might want to give WinPython a try. This distribution offers similar features as the ones we discussed earlier, however it is community driven. This means that it's an open source tool that is entirely free.

You can also install multiple versions of it on the same machine, and it comes with an IDE pre-installed.

Virtual Environments

Virtual environments are often necessary because you are usually locked to the version of Python you installed. It doesn't matter whether you installed everything manually or you chose to use a distribution - you can't have as many installations on the same machine as you might want. The only exception would be if you are using the WinPython distribution, which is available only for Windows machines, because it allow you to prepare as many installations as you want. However, you can create a virtual environment with the "virtualenv".

23

Create as many different installations as you need without worrying about any kind of limitations. Here are a few solid reasons why you should choose a virtual environment:

- Testing grounds: It allows you to create a special environment where you can experiment with different libraries, modules, Python versions and so on. This way, you can test anything you can think of without causing any irreversible damage.

- Different versions: There are cases when you need multiple installations of Python on your computer. There are packages and tools, for instance, that only work with a certain version. For instance, if you are running Windows, there are a few useful packages that will only behave correctly if you are running Python 3.4, which isn't the most recent update. Through a virtual environment, you can run different version of Python for separate goals.

- Replicability: Use a virtual environment to make sure you can run your project on any other computer or version of Python aside from the one you were originally using. You might be required to run your prototype on a certain operating system or Python installation, instead of the one you are using on your own computer. With the help of a virtual environment, you can easily replicate your project and see if it runs under different circumstances.

With that being said, let's start installing a virtual environment by typing the following command:

pip install virtualenv

This will install "virtualenv", however you will first need to make several preparations before creating the virtual environment. Here are some of the decisions you have to make at the end of the installation process:

- Python version: Decide which version you want "virtualenv" to use. By default, it will pick up the one it was installed from. Therefore, if you want to use another Python version, you have to specify by typing -p python 3.4, for instance.

- Package installation: The virtual environment tool is set to always perform the full package installation process for each environment even when you already have said package installed on your system. This can lead to a loss of time and resources. To avoid this issue, you can use the --system-site-packages command to instruct the tool to install the packages from the files already available on your system.

- Relocation: For some projects, you might need to move your virtual environment on a different Python setup or even on another computer. In that case, you will have to instruct the tool to make the environment scripts work on any path. This can be achieved with the --relocatable command.

Once you make all the above decisions, you can finally create a new environment. Type the following command:

virtualenv myenv

This instruction will create a new directory called "myenv" inside the location, or directory, where you currently are. Once the virtual environment is created, you need to launch it by typing these lines:

cd myenv

activate

Now you can start installing various packages by using any package manager like we discussed earlier in the chapter.

Necessary Packages

We discussed earlier that the advantages of using Python for data science are its system compatibility and highly developed system of packages. An aspiring data scientist will require a diverse set of tools for their projects. The analytical packages we are going to talk about have been highly polished and thoroughly tested over the years, and therefore are used by the majority of data scientists, analysts, and engineers.

Here are the most important packages you will need to install for most of your work:

- NumPy: This analytical library provides the user with support for multi-dimensional arrays, including the mathematical algorithms needed to operate on them. Arrays are used for storing data, as well as for fast matrix operations that are much needed to work out many data science problems. Python wasn't meant for numerical computing, therefore every data scientist needs a package like NumPy to extend the programming language to include the use of many high level mathematical functions. Install this tool by typing the following command: pip install numpy.

- SciPy: You can't read about NumPy without hearing about SciPy. Why? Because the two complement each other. SciPy is needed to enable the use of algorithms for image processing, linear algebra, matrices and more. Install this tool by typing the following command: pip install scipy.

- pandas: This library is needed mostly for handling diverse data tables. Install pandas to be able to load data from any source and manipulate as needed. Install this tool by typing the following command: pip install pandas.

- Scikit-learn: A much needed tool for data science and machine learning, Scikit is probably the most important package in your toolkit. It is required for data preprocessing, error metrics, supervised and unsupervised learning, and much more. Install this tool by typing the following command: pip install scikit-learn.

- Matplotlib: This package contains everything you need to build plots from an array. You also have the ability to visualize them interactively. You don't happen to know what a plot is? It is a graph used in statistics and data analysis to display the relation between variables. This makes Matplotlib an indispensable library for Python. Install this tool by typing the following command: pip install matplotlib.

- Jupyter: No data scientist is complete without Jupyter. This package is essentially an IDE (though much more) used in data science and machine learning everywhere. Unlike IDEs such as Atom, or R Studio, Jupyter can be used with any programming language. It is both powerful and

29

versatile because it provides the user with the ability to perform data visualization in the same environment, and allows customizable commands. Not only that, it also promotes collaboration due to its streamlined method of sharing documents. Install this tool by typing the following command: pip install jupyter.

- Beautiful Soup: Extract information from HTML and XML files that you have access to online. Install this tool by typing the following command: pip install beautifulsoup4.

For now, these 7 packages should be enough to get you started and give you an idea on how to extend Python's abilities. You don't have to overwhelm yourself just yet by installing all of them, however feel free to explore and experiment on your own. We will mention and discuss more packages later in the book as needed to solve our data science problems. But for now, we need to focus more on Jupyter, because it will be used throughout the book. So let's go through the installation, special commands, and learn how this tool can help you as an aspiring data scientist.

Using Jupyter

Throughout this book, we will use Jupyter to illustrate various operations we perform and their results. If you didn't install it yet, let's start by typing the following command:

pip install jupyter

The installation itself is straightforward. Simply follow the steps and instruction you receive during the setup process. Just make sure to download the correct installer first. Once the setup finishes, we can run the program by typing the next line:

jupyter notebook

This will open an instance of Jupyter inside your browser. Next, click on "New" and select the version of Python you are running. As mentioned earlier, we are going to focus on Python 3. Now you will see an empty window where you can type your commands.

You might notice that Jupyter uses code cell blocks instead of looking like a regular text editor. That's because the program will execute code cell by cell. This allows you to test and experiment with parts of your code instead of your entire program. With that being said, let's give it a test run and type the following line inside the cell:

In: print ("I'm running a test!")

Now you can click on the play button that is located under the Cell tab. This will run your code and give you an output, and then a new input cell will appear. You can also create more cells by hitting the plus button in the menu. To make it clearer, a typical block looks something like this:

In: < This is where you type your code >

Out: < This is the output you will receive >

The idea is to type your code inside the "In" section and then run it. You can optionally type in the result you expect to receive inside the "Out" section, and when you run the code, you will see another "Out" section that displays the true result. This way you can also test to see if the code gives you the result you expect.

Data science and artificial intelligence

Machine Learning will study an algorithm and let machines recognize patterns, develop models, and generate videos and images via learning. Machine Learning algorithms can be created using different methods such as clustering, decision trees, linear regression, and many more.

What is an Artificial Neural Network?

Artificial Neural Network is propelled by biological models of brain and biological neural networks. In brief, Artificial Neural Network (ANN) refers to a computational representation of the human neural network which alters human intelligence, memory, and reasoning. But why should the human brain system develop effective ML algorithms? The major principle behind ANN is that neural networks are effective in advanced computations and hierarchical representation of knowledge. Dendrites and axons connect neurons into complex neural networks that can pass and exchange information as well as store intermediary computation results. Therefore, a computational model of such systems can be effective in learning processes that resemble biological ones.

The perception algorithm created in 1957 was the trial to build a computational model of a biological neural network. However, advanced neural networks that have multiple layers, neurons, and nodes became possible just recently. ANN is the reason for the recent success in computer vision and image recognition. Natural Language Processing and other applications of machine language seek to extract complex patterns from data. Neural networks are very useful when one wants to study nonlinear hypothesis that has many features. Building a precise hypothesis for a massive feature space may need one to have multiple high order polynomials that would inevitably result in overfitting. This is a situation where a model reveals random noise in data instead of the underlying patterns of relationships. The issue with overfitting involves image recognition problems. Here, each pixel represents a feature. A Simple Neural Network That Has a Single Neuron The simplest neural network has a single 'neuron'. By applying a biological analogy, this neuron represents a computational unit that assumes inputs through electrical inputs and transfers them using axons to the next network output.

Data science tips and tricks

One of the major strengths of Data Scientists is a strong background in Math and Statistics. Mathematics helps them create complex analytics. Besides this, they also use mathematics to create Machine Learning models and Artificial Intelligence. Similar to software engineering, Data Scientists must interact with the business side. This involves mastering the domain so that they can draw insights. Data Scientists need to analyze data to help a business, and this calls for some business acumen. Lastly, the results need to be assigned to the business in a way that anyone can understand. This calls for the ability to verbally and visually communicate advanced results and observations in a manner that a business can understand as well as work on it.

Therefore, it is important for any wannabe Data Scientists to have knowledge about Data Mining. Data Mining describes the process where raw data is structured in such a way where one can recognize patterns in the data via mathematical and computational algorithms.

Below are five mining techniques that every data scientist should know:

1. MapReduce The modern Data Mining applications need to manage vast amounts of data rapidly.

To deal with these applications, one must use a new software stack. Since programming systems can retrieve parallelism from a computing cluster, a software stack has a new file system called a distributed file system. The system has a larger unit than the disk blocks found in the normal operating system. A distributed file system replicates data to enforce security against media failures. In addition to such file systems, a higher-level programming system has also been created. This is referred to as MapReduce. It is a form of computing which has been implemented in different systems such as Hadoop and Google's implementation. You

can adopt a MapReduce implementation to control large-scale computations such that it can deal with hardware faults. You only need to write three functions. That is Map and Reduce, and then you can allow the system to control parallel execution and task collaboration.

2. Distance Measures

The major problem with Data Mining is reviewing data for similar items. An example can be searching for a collection of web pages and discovering duplicate pages. Some of these pages could be plagiarism or pages that have almost identical content but different in content. Other examples can include customers who buy similar products or discover images with similar characteristics. Distance measure basically refers to a technique that handles this problem. It searches for the nearest neighbors in a higher dimensional space. For every application, it is important to define the meaning of similarity. The most popular definition is the Jaccard Similarity. It refers to the ratio between intersection sets and union. It is the best similarity to reveal textual similarity found in documents and certain behaviors of customers.

For example, when looking for identical documents, there are different instances of this particular example. There might be very many small pieces of one document appearing out of order, more documents for comparisons, and documents that are so large to fit in the main memory. To handle these issues, there are three important steps to finding similar documents.

• Shingling. This involves converting documents into sets.

• Min-Hashing. It involves converting a large set into short signatures while maintaining similarity.

• Locality Sensitive Hashing. Concentrate on signature pairs that might be from similar documents. The most powerful way that you can represent documents assets is to retrieve a set of short strings from the document.

• A k-Shingle refers to any k characters that can show up in a document.

• A min-hash functions on sets.

• Locality-Sensitive Hashing.

3. Link Analysis

Traditional search engines did not provide accurate search results because of spam vulnerability. However, Google managed to overcome this problem by using the following technique:

• PageRank. It uses simulation. If a user surfing a web page starts from a random page, PageRank attempts to congregate in case it had monitored specific outlines from the page that users are located. This whole process works iteratively meaning pages that have a higher number of users are ranked better than pages without users visiting.

• The content in a page was determined by the specific phrases used in the page and linked with external pages. Although it is easy for a spammer to modify a page that they are administrators, it is very difficult for them to do the same on an external page which they aren't administrators.

In other words, PageRank represents a function that allocates a real number to a web page. The intention is that a page with a higher page rank becomes more important than a page that does not have a page rank.

There is no fixed algorithm defined to assign a page rank, but there are different varieties.

For powerfully connected Web Graphs, PageRank applies the principle of the transition matrix. This principle is useful for calculating the rank of a page.

To calculate the behavior of a page rank, it simulates the actions of random users on a page.

There are different enhancements that one can make to PageRank. The first one is called Topic-Sensitive PageRank. This type of improvement can weigh certain pages more heavily as a result of their topic. If you are aware of the query on a particular page, then it is possible to be based on the rank of the page.

4. Data Streaming

In most of the Data Mining situations, you can't know the whole data set in advance. There are times when data arrives in the form of a stream, and then gets processed immediately before it disappears forever. Furthermore, the speed at which data arrives very fast, and that makes it hard to store in the active storage. In short, the data is infinite and non-stationary. Stream management, therefore, becomes very important.

In the data stream management system, there is no limit to the number of streams that can fit into a system. Each data stream produces elements at its own time. The elements should then have the same data rates and time in a particular stream.

Streams can be archived into a store, but this will make it impossible to reply to queries from the archival store. This can later be analyzed under special cases by using a specific retrieval method.

Furthermore, there is a working store where summaries are placed so that one can use to reply to queries. The active store can either be a disk or main memory. It all depends on the speed at which one wants to process the queries. Whichever way, it does not have the right capacity to store data from other streams.

Data streaming has different problems as highlighted below: • Sampling Data in a Stream

To create a sample of the stream that is used in a class of queries, you must select a set of attributes to be used in a stream. By hashing the key of an incoming stream element, the hash value can be the best to help determine whether all or none of the elements in the key belong to the sample.

• Filtering Streams

To accept tuples that fit a specific criterion, accepted tuples should go through a separate process of the stream while the rest of the tuples are eliminated. Bloom filtering is a wonderful technique that one can use to filter streams to allow elements in a given set to pass through while foreign elements are deleted. Members in the selected set are hashed into buckets to form bits. The bits are then set to 1. If you would like to test an element of a stream, you must hash the element into a set of bits using the hash function.

• Count Specific Elements in a Stream

Consider stream elements chosen from a universal set. If you wanted to know the number of unique elements that exist in a stream, you might have to count from the start of the stream. Flajolet-Martin is a method which often hashes elements to integers, described as binary numbers. By using a lot of the hash functions and integrating these estimates, you finally get a reliable estimate.

5. Frequent Item – Set Analysis

The market-basket model features many relationships. On one side, there are items, and on the opposite side, there are baskets. Every basket contains a set of items. The hypothesis created here is that the number of items in the basket is always smaller than the total number of items. This means that if you count the items in the basket, it should be high and large to fit in memory. Here, data is similar to a file that has a series of baskets. In reference to the distributed file system, baskets represent the original file. Each basket is of type "set of items".

As a result, a popular family technique to characterize data depending on the market-basket model is to discover frequent item-sets. These are sets of items that reveal the most baskets. Market basket analysis was previously applied in supermarket and chain stores. These stores track down the contents of each market basket that a customer brings to the checkout. Items represent products sold by the store while baskets are a set of items found in a single basket. That said, this same model can be applied in many different data types such as:

• Similar concepts. Let items represent words and baskets documents. Therefore, a document or basket has words or items available in the document. If you were to search for words that are repeated in a document, sets would contain the most words. • • Plagiarism. You can let the items represent documents and baskets to be sentenced. Properties of Frequent-Item Sets to Know • Association rules. These refer to implications in case a basket has a specific set of items.

• Monotonicity. One of the most important properties of item-sets is that if a set is frequent, then all its subsets are frequent.

Chapter 2: Basic fundamentals of Python

While we are on the topic of the Python language, we need to spend some time looking at some of the basics that come with this language. The Python language is relatively easy to learn about and work with, so that should be welcome news to those who are brand new into coding and have not been able to work with it in the past. With this in mind, let's dive in a bit and learn more about how to work with the Python language.

The Python Keywords

First, we are going to start with the Python keywords. These keywords are reserved to tell the compiler command. You do not want to use them anywhere else in the code, and you must make sure that you use them properly. If you try to use the keyword in the wrong place of the code, it will result in an error.

These keywords are there to give commands to the compiler so that it knows how it should react to your code. They are important to the code and to the compiler so make sure to only use them where they are needed and as a command to the compiler

How to Name an Identifier

The next thing that we need to take a look at when it comes to our own coding is how to name the identifiers. These identifiers are important in the code and there are actually quite a few of these identifiers that we need to pay attention to when we work on this kind of coding language. You will find that they come in different names, and you may see them as things like classes, entities, functions, and variables to name a few when you are ready to name one of your identifiers, you can use the same information, as well as the same rules, when you name each of them. This can make it a bit easier to remember rather than having different rules for each type. Now, the first rule that we have to focus on when it comes to these identifiers is that there are a lot of options and you are pretty free here. You are able to work with all kinds of letters,whether they are uppercase or lowercase or a combination of the two. Numbers and the underscore symbol are also allowed

46

as well. You can combine all of these characters together as well.

One thing to remember when we are going to name these identifiers is that you are not able to start the name of one of them with a number, and you never want to have a space between the words that you are writing. So something like 4birds or four birds would not be allowed, but writing out four birds or four_birds would be just fine.

While it is not necessarily one of the rules that you have to follow, something to consider when you are naming these is to go with a name that you will be able to remember. This makes it easier to find that identifier and call it back out later on if you would like to use it in the code. It just makes things easier when it makes sense for the part of the code that you are in, and that it is something you can remember later.

The Python Statements

We can also spend a moment on the Python statements. These are pretty simple to work with, but it is still a good idea to spend some time looking at them and seeing how they all fit together to do the work that you would like.

So, to explore this further, the statements are going to be the strings of code that you write out and that you would like the compiler to show up on your screen. When you give the instructions over to the compiler for what you want the statements to say, it is going to put that information up on the screen. As long as you write them out properly, then the compiler will make sure that the message you are asking for will be on the screen and ready to go on time. it is as

simple as that!

The Comments

As you are writing out the code, you may find that there are times you want to include a little note or a little explanation of what you are writing inside the code. These are little notes that you and other programmers are able to read through in the code and can help explain out what you are doing with that part of the code. Any comment that you write out in Python will need to use the # symbol ahead of it. This tells the compiler that you are writing out a comment and that it should move on to the next block of code.

You can add in as many of these comments as you need to explain the code that you are writing and to help it make sense. You could have one very another line if you would like, but you should try not to add in too many or you may make a mess of the code that you have. But as long as the # symbol is in front of the statement, you can write out as many of these comments as you would like and your compiler will just skip out of them.

Bringing In the Python Variables

The next thing on the list that we can explore is the Python variables. These are another important part of the code that we need to spend some time on, mainly because they show up in the code so much and are so common, that you will see them quite a bit.

These variables are going to show up in your code in order to help store and hold onto the values that are important to helping your code function in the right manner. This helps everything to stay as nice and organized as you would like.

You can easily add in some of the values to the right variable as you would like, and it only takes adding in the equal sign between both of them.

The Operators

Operators are pretty simple parts of your code, but you should still know how they work. You will find that there are actually a few different types of them that work well. For example, the arithmetic functions are great for helping you to add, divide, subtract, and multiply different parts of the code together.

The Python Functions

Another topic that we need to take a moment to explore with this language is known as the Python functions. These functions can basically be a set of expressions, and sometimes they are given the name of statements, that are capable of being named or being kept anonymous depending on what you would like to see done with your code. These are going to be some of the very first-in-class objects for the code, which means that you are not going to spend a lot of time worrying about the restrictions that come with these. When working on these Python functions, you will be able to use them in a manner that is similar to other values, including values like strings and numbers, and they will have other attributes that we are able to pull out and use in any manner that we would like. The good news with the functions is that they are pretty diversified to work with, and there are a lot of different attributes that we are able to use in order to create and then bring out these functions. Some of the choices that we can have with these kinds of functions include some of the following:

__doc__: This is going to return the docstring of the function that you are requesting.

Func_default: This one is going to return a tuple of the values of your default argument.

Func_globals: This one will return a reference that points to the dictionary holding the global variables for that function.

Func_dict: This one is responsible for returning the namespace that will support the attributes for all your arbitrary functions.

Func_closure: This will return to you a tuple of all the cells that hold the bindings for the free variables inside of the function.

Now, keep in mind here that there are going to be a few different things that we are able to do with these functions, such as bringing them out to pass an argument from one function to another, as needed.

Any function that is able to take on a new one as the argument is going to be the higher-order function in our code.

The Python Classes

No discussion on the basics of Python will be complete without a discussion about the classes. These are going to be all about how the code in Python is organized, and how we can make sure that the parts come together and do what we would like in the end. These classes are going to be simple containers in the code that can hold onto the objects that we want to hold onto in our code.

We have to make sure that the naming of the classes is done right and then put the objects in them the right way, but this can ensure that the classes are going to work the way that we want. The neat thing about these classes is that they can hold onto and store anything that we would like. But keep in mind that the objects that are in one class make sense that they go with one another, and won't confuse others as to why they show up together. The items don't have to turn out to be identical at all, but they do need to make sense with each other. You could have a class of food, vehicles, or colors if you would like, but they do need to make sense of how they go together.

Classes are going to be very important when it is time to write out one of the codes that we would like to use. These classes are responsible for holding onto the various objects that we would like to work with. They can also ensure that it is easier to bring out all of the different parts of our code when we need them to execute and behave the way that we would like them to.

As you can see, there are a lot of different parts that will come together to write out a good code in the Python language.

They are sometimes a bit hard to get started on, and it may seem like a lot of information. But in reality, all of this goes together and makes the coding easier than ever before. Make sure to learn these parts and understand how they go with one another so that you can start writing out some of your very own codes in no time.

Control flow

Another thing that we need to spend a moment looking at is the control flow that happens in Python. This is important to make sure that we are able to write out the codes that we want in the Python language. There are going to be some types of strings that are going to be inside the code, and you may choose to write these out in a manner so that the compiler is able to read and execute them in the right manner.

But if you do not write out the string in the right manner, then the compiler is going to send out an error in the system. We are going to spend some of our time looking at a variety of codes in this guidebook, and they will help us to learn a bit more about the control flow that Python would like us to follow. This makes it easier for us to know what we need to get done, and how you are able to write out codes.

Chapter 3: Python Data Types

There are a lot of different types of data in Python. Some of the crucial data types that we are able to work with includes:

Python numbers

The first option that we are able to work on Python data includes the Python numbers. These are going to include things like complex numbers, floating-point numbers, and even integers. They are going to be defined as complex, float, and int classes in Python. For example, we are able to work with the type() function to identify which category a value or a variable affiliated with to, and then the isinstance() function to audit if an object exists to a distinct class.

When we work with integers can be of any length, it is going to only find limitations in how much memory you have available on your computer. Then there is the floating-point number.

This is going to be accurate up to 15 decimal places, though you can definitely go with a smaller amount as well.

The floating points are going to be separated by a decimal point. 1 is going to be an integer, and 10 will be a floating-point number.

And finally, we have complex numbers. These are going to be the numbers that we will want to write out as x + y, where x is going to be the real point, and then they are going to be the imaginary part. We need to have these two put together in order to make up the complexity that we need with this kind of number.

Python lists

The next type of data that will show up in the Python language. The Python list is going to be a regulated series of items. It is going to be one of the data types that are used the most in Python, and it is exceedingly responsive.

All of the items that will show up on the list can be similar, but this is not a requirement. You are able to work with a lot of different items on your list, without them being the same type, to make it easier to work with.

Being able to declare a list is going to be a straightforward option that we are able to work with. The items are going to be separated out by commas and then we just need to include them inside some brackets like this: [ ] we can also employ the slicing operator to help us obtain out a piece or a selection of items out of that list. The index starts at 0 in Python. And we have to remember while working on these that lists are going to be mutable. What this means is that the value of the elements that are on your list can be altered in order to meet your own needs overall.

Python Tuple

We can also work with something that is known as a Python Tuple. The Tuple is going to be an ordered series of components that is the duplicate as a list, and it is sometimes hard to see how these are going to be similar and how they are going to be different. The gigantic diverse that we are going to see with a Tuple and a list is that the tuples are going to be immutable. Tuples, once you create them, are not modifiable.

Tuples are applied to write-protect data, and we are generally quicker than a list, as they cannot shift actively. It is going to be determined with parentheses () where the items are also going to be separated out by a comma as we see with the lists.

We can then use the slicing operator to help us wring some of the components that we want to use, but we still are not able to change the value while we are working with the code or the program.

Python Strings

In Python, strings can be seen as a connected series of characters represented within quotes, which can either be single or double pairs. To take the subset of a string, the slice operator ([]) and ([:]) are used, with indexes beginning at 0 from the starting of the string and working their way from -1 at the terminal point.

Python dictionary

In Python, dictionaries refer to some sort of hash table type.

The function in the same way as the hashes or associative arrays peculiar to Perl programming, and are made up of key-value pairs. A dictionary key can be about any type in Python, but they usually take the form of strings or numbers. On the other hand, values can be used as any arbitrary object in Python.

Chapter 4: Data Science with Python

Introduction to NumPy; packages installations; manipulating array; conditional selection; etc.

NumPy is short from for Numerical Python, and it is one of the *more significant foundational packages used for numerical* computing of Python. Almost all computational packages provide scientific functionality by using NumPy array objects like lingua franca used for data exchange. Here are the things you can use with NumPy.

- ndarray which is an efficient multidimensional array which provides a fast array oriented arithmetic operation with flexible broadcasting capabilities.

- Math functions used for quick operations on the entire array of data without the requirement for writing loops.

- Tools for reading and writing the array data to a disk and working by using memory and mapped files.

- Capabilities are provided for random number generation, linear algebra, and Fourier transformation.

- A C API used for connecting the NumPy with libraries developed by using C, C++, and FORTRON.

A simple to use C API is provided by NumPy, and so it is straightforward to pass the data to external libraries written in lower level languages. It also enables the external libraries to return data as NumPy arrays to Python. This feature makes Python the language of choice for wrapping of legacy C/C++/FORTRAN code bases and providing them a simple, dynamic, and easy-to-use interface.

Although NumPy does not give scientific or modeling functionalities, being blessed with the understanding of NumPy arrays along with the array-oriented computing will aid you in using tools having array-oriented semantics such as Pandas a lot more effectively. As NumPy is a big topic, we will cover the fundamental features here. We will see the main functional areas related to data analytics in this chapter. These include

- Quick Vectorized array operation used for data munging and cleaning, transformation, subsetting and filtering, and other types of computations.

- Usual array algorithms used such as unique, sorting, and set operations.

- Efficient descriptive aggregating and statistics and summarizing the data.

- Relational data manipulations and data alignment for joining and merging the heterogeneous datasets together.

- Expressing of conditional logic as array expressions rather than loops having if-elif-else branches.

- Group-wise data manipulation such as transformation, aggregation, and function application.

Although NumPy provides a computational foundation for normal numerical data processing, several users wish to use pandas as their basis for almost all kinds of analytics and statistics, especially in the case of tabular data. Pandas will also provide greater domain specific functionalities such as time series manipulation that is not there in NumPy.

Remember that the Python array-oriented computing goes way back to 1995 when the Numeric library was created by Jim Hugunin. Over the period of next 10 years, several scientific programming communities started doing array programming by using Python.

One of the main reasons why the NumPy is so significant towards the numerical computations of Python is that it is designed for efficiency regarding the large data arrays. You can find a number of reasons for it such as these,

- There is a contiguous block of memory available in NumPy where it stores the memory independent of other Python objects that are available built-in. The NumPy library containing algorithms is written in C and can operate on this particular memory with no type checking or other overheads. The NumPy arrays utilize a lot less memory than compared to the built-in Python sequences.

- Complex computations can be performed by NumPy on the entire arrays without needing Python for the loops.

For providing an idea regarding the difference in performance, you can consider the NumPy array with a million integers and an equivalent Python list.

In [7]: import numpy as np

In [8]: our_arr = np.arange(1000000)

In [9]: my_list = list(range(1000000))

Now, let's multiple every sequence by 2.

In [10]: %time for _ in range(10): our_array2 = our_arr * 2

CPU times: user 20 ms, sys: 10 ms, total: 30 ms

Wall time: 31.3 ms

In [11]: %time for _ in range(10): my_list2 = [x * 2 for x in my_list]

CPU times: user 680 ms, sys: 180 ms, total: 860 ms

Wall time: 861 ms

The NumPy-based algorithms are normally ten to a hundred times quicker than their Python counterparts, and they use substantially less memory.

ndarray of NumPy! The multidimensional array object!

NumPy has many features, and one of the key ones is the ndarray (N-dimensional array object) ndarray. It is a quick and flexible container for the large datasets of Python. The arrays enable you to do mathematical operations on whole sets of data by using a syntax similar to the equivalent operations of scalar elements. For providing you an idea about how the NumPy facilitates batch computations by using similar syntax to that of the scalar values of built-in Python objects, you will first have to import NumPy and develop a small array containing random data.

In [12]: import numpy as np

Generate some random data

In [13]: data = np.random.randn(2, 3)

In [14]: data

Out[14]:

array([[-0.2047, 0.4789, -0.5194],

[-0.5557, 1.9658, 1.3934]])

Then we will write the mathematical operations of the data,

In [15]: data * 10

Out[15]:

array([[-2.0471, 4.7894, -5.1944],

[-5.5573, 19.6578, 13.9341]])

In [16]: data + data

Out[16]:

array([[-0.4094, 0.9579, -1.0389],

[-1.1115, 3.9316, 2.7868]])

In your first instance, all the code elements are multiplied by 10. And in the 2nd, the corresponding values of every cell of the array are added to each other. Remember, in this chapter the standard NumPy convention is used as np for import numpy. The reader is welcome to use from numpy import * for your code to avoid writing "np." However, you are advised against making a habit of it. The namespace numpy is big and consists of a number of functions having names that conflict with the built-in Python functions such as min and max.

The ndarray is a generic and multidimensional homogeneous data container. It means that all its elements have to be of the same type. Each array comes with a shape and a tuple, which indicates the size of every dimension. It also comes with a dtype, and an object describing the data type of an array.

Creating ndarrays

The simplest way of creating an array by using the array function. It accepts all sequence like objects including other arrays and produces new NumPy arrays containing passed data. For instance, the list is a good candidate for converting.

In [19]: data1 = [6, 7.5, 8, 0, 1]

In [20]: array1 = np.array(data1)

In [21]: array1

Out[21]: array([6. , 7.5, 8. , 0. , 1.])

Nested sequences such as a list containing other equal-length lists can be converted into multidimensional arrays.

In [22]: data2 = [[1, 2, 3, 4], [5, 6, 7, 8]]

In [23]: array2 = np.array(data2)

In [24]: array2

Out[24]:

array([[1, 2, 3, 4],

[5, 6, 7, 8]])

Here as data2 was a list containing other lists, NumPy array array2 has 2 dimensions with the shape inferred from data. You can confirm it by inspecting ndim and shape attributes.

In [25]: array2.ndim

Out[25]: 2

In [26]: array2.shape

Out[26]: (2, 4)

Unless it is explicitly specified the np.array will try to infer a good data type for an array which it creates. A data type is stored in special dtype metadata object for instance. For instance in the examples specified above we have,

In [27]: array1.dtype

Out[27]: dtype('float64')

In [28]: array2.dtype

Out[28]: dtype('int64')

In addition to the np.array you can find a number of other functions for the creation of new arrays. For example, zeros and ones can create arrays of 0s and 1s respectively with provided shape or length. An "empty" will create an array without initializing a value to a specific value. For creating a high dimensional array by using these methods you can pass a tuple for a shape,

In [29]: np.zeros(10)

Out[29]:
array([0., 0., 0., 0., 0., 0., 0., 0., 0., 0.])

In [30]: np.zeros((3, 6))

Out[30]:

array([[0., 0., 0., 0., 0., 0.],

[0., 0., 0., 0., 0., 0.],

[0., 0., 0., 0., 0., 0.]])

In [31]: np.empty((2, 3, 2))

Out[31]:

array([[[0., 0.],

[0., 0.],

[0., 0.]],

[[0., 0.],

[0., 0.],

[0., 0.]]])

It is not safe to assume here that the np.empty can return an array containing all zeros. In many cases it will return uninitialized garbage values. An "arrange" happens to be the array valued version of a built-in "range" function of Python.

In [32]: np.arange(15)

Out[32]: array([0, 1, 2, 3, 4, 5, 6, 7, 8, 9, 10, 11, 12, 13, 14])

You can see the standard array creation functions in the table below. As NumPy concentrates on numerical computing its data type in case it is not specified will be float64 (floating point) in many cases.

Data types required for ndarrays

A dtype or data type is a special object which contains information or metadata. This is required by the ndarray for interpreting memory chunks as a specific kind of data.

In [33]: array1 = np.array([1, 2, 3], dtype=np.float64)

In [34]: array2 = np.array([1, 2, 3], dtype=np.int32)

In [35]: array1.dtype

Out[35]: dtype('float64')

In [36]: array2.dtype

Out[36]: dtype('int32')[9]

Dtypes happen to be the source for the NumPy flexibility while interacting with the data that comes from other systems. In almost all cases, they will provide mapping directly on the underlying disks or memory representation. It makes things easy for reading and writing binary streams of data to the disk and also for connecting to the code written in any low-level language such as FORTRON or C. Numeric dtypes are named in a similar manner. They have a type name such as an int or a float which is followed by a number which indicates the number of bits per every element. Any standard double precision float value of the kind used under the Python hood of the floating object takes up 8 or 64 bits. Therefore the type is called as float64 in NumPy. Look at the table below for the full listing of data types supported by NumPy. But do not bother memorizing the NumPy dtypes especially in case you are a new user. Often it is necessary to take care of the general data you are handling whether it is complex, Boolean, floating point, integer, string, or another general Python object. In case you want to control how data is put into storage, then you can pick the storage type for it with ease in python.

Manipulating array

Now it is time for us to take a look at how we are able to work with some of the arrays that are in our midst and how these are going to be important to unlocking some of the power that we are going to be able to work with when it comes to the arrays and the NumPy library.

Like many of the other data science libraries that are out there and will work with Python as well, NumPy is going to be one of the packages that we just can't miss out on when it is time to learn more about data science along the way. This is because NumPy is going to be able to provide us with some of the data structure that we need with arrays that will hold a few benefits over the list with Python. For example, the arrays are going to be more

compact, they can access faster when it is time to read and write the items, and they are more efficient and convenient to work with overall.

With this in mind, we are going to spend some time looking at how to work with the NumPy arrays. We are going to look at how to work with these, how they can be installed, and even how to make some of the arrays that we would like to work with, even when you need to work with the data when it is on the files.

The NumPy Array

The first thing that we are going to take a look at here is the NumPy array. The arrays that come from this library are going to be similar to the lists that we are going to find in Python, but there are some differences that are going to show up. The array is going to be one of the central structures of data that are found in the NumPy library. In other words, the NumPy library is going to be one of the core libraries that we need to work with when it is time to do some scientific computing, and the arrays are going to be central to getting things done in this library as well.

When we take a look at the print of a few arrays, you are going to see that it is more of a grid that will hold onto values that are the same type. You will then see that the data is often going to be in integers. The array is going to help us out by holding and representing any regular data that has been structured in this manner.

However, we are going to be aware that, on a structural level, an array is basically going to be nothing but pointers. It is going to be a combination of the memory address, shapes, strides, and a data type. Some of the things that we need to know when we go through this process include:

1.The data pointer is going to be important in order to indicate the memory address that we are going to find with the first byte of this particular array.

2.Then we are able to work with the dtype, or the data type. This pointer is going to describe the kind of elements that we are able to find inside of the array that we are working with.

3.Then we move on to the shape. This is going to give us a better idea of the shape that our array is going to take.

4.And finally, we are on the strides. These will basically be the number of bytes that we are able to skip in the memory so that we can then go on to the next elements.

So, if you end up with strides of (10, 1), you will need to proceed one byte in order to get to the next column, and 10 bytes so that they are in the next row.

To put this in other words, an array is going to be able to contain a lot of information about the data that is raw, how to find the element that we are able to work with, and how we are able to interpret the specific element that we would like to work with.

Now we are able to take this a bit further to see how it is going to work for some of our needs.

This is going to be much more detailed than we find before. This also means that we are going to store the array in memory as 64 bytes. This is because each integer is going to take up to 8 bytes, and you are going to work here with an array that has 8 integers.

The strides that we are going to see with the array are able to tell us that it is important for us to skip 8 bytes, which is one value here, to move to the next column when it is needed. But if we are working with the 32 bytes, which would be four values, to get to the same position in the next row. The strides that we would sce with this kind of array is going to be (32, 4).

Note that if we set up the type of data on this one to be int32, then the strides tuple that you are able to get back is going to be (16, 4), as you will still just need to move one value to the next column and 4 values to get to the same potion. The only thing that we will need to change up here is the fact that all of the integers will take up 4 bytes rather than the 8 that you are expecting at this time.

As we can see, working with the arrays is pretty simple, but it is going to be important when it is time to handle some o the work that we are trying to do with our Python and with data science in the same process. When we are able to handle all of this at the same time and put it together, you will find that it works with a lot of options with the other data science libraries that we would like to work with as well.

Chapter 5: Manipulating data with the Pandas library

You will find that the Pandas library is one of the best data analysis libraries, and it is going to take some time to handle all of the different aspects of the data analysis process. This is one of the reasons why we need to take some time to download this library and get it set up to work with Python so that you can handle your work with data analysis.

With this in mind, it is time for us to move on and learn how we are able to set up and install the Pandas library on your system. This is a simple process that we are able to work with, and it is not meant to be complicated. But we do need to take a look at some of the different steps that are needed in order to load and then save Pandas and get it ready to use on your system.

How to Install Pandas

The first thing that we are going to take a look at is the steps, and the coding, that we need to do in order to get Pandas ready to go and installed on our system. To make sure that we are able to use Pandas, it needs to first be installed on our computer. We are going to make the assumption that you went through the steps needed earlier in order to get Python all set up and ready to go with your system, so that will save some of the time and energy that we need to use for this process right now.

To get us started with this, we need to check what version of Python we are working with. If you decided to download Python recently, then it is likely that you are working with a version of Python 3, and that will work just fine with Pandas. But if you have been working with Python for some time and installed it a long time ago on your system, then it is important to check which version. Pandas works with any version of Python that is Python 2.7 or higher so make sure that you have a version that fits or updates which type of Python you are working with.

Once we are certain that we are working with a new enough version of the Python library to get the work done, it is time to take a look at some of the libraries that are available to work with as well. We have to make sure that the NumPy library is present on our system because this library is going to be able to work with the NumPy arrays. Without NumPy on our system already, the Pandas library is not going to do what we would like.

We also have some optional libraries that we are able to work within this library as well. The Matplotlib library is a great option, especially when it is time to work with some plotting or with a few of the visuals that are helpful with our data analysis.

This is a great option to work with because it helps us to go through and get all of those libraries in one place. Rather than having to go through and download all of these extensions and libraries one by one, we are able to go through and install them at once through the Anaconda distribution, or through another similar kind of distribution as well. This will allow us to download all of this to Windows, Mac, and Linux versions. If you would like to install it in a different manner, then we are going to go through the steps and the coding that will help you to get all of this done.

To make sure that we are able to get Pandas to work on your system and to make sure that it is going to be compatible with your Python IDE means that we need to import this library first. Importing the Pandas library is easier than you may think in the beginning, because it just means that we are going to load the library into the memory, and then it is there for you to bring out and work with any time that you would like.

Usually, we need to make sure that we are able to go through and add in the second part of both lines above in order to make it easier to bring up some of the parts that we want to do with coding later on. For example, with the pd part, we are able to write out something like pd.command rather than having to go through and write out pandas. command each time that we would like to use this.

As we can see above as well, we are able to import the NumPy library. Remember that we talked about how this library is going to be an important one to work with because Pandas needs to have the NumPy arrays around in order to finish some of the scientific computing that comes with our data analysis and machine learning. At this point, if you were able to go through the process properly and everything is ready, you can start to work with the Pandas library. Remember, you will need to use that two-line code from above each time that you start up the Python IDE, whether it is a Spyder file, a Jupyter Notebook, or something else similar along the way. this ensures that the compiler and the Notebook know that you would like to use that to see the best results with your work.

Chapter 6: Machine learning with Python

Any time that we are ready to handle data analysis, it is important that we take some time to explore the basics of machine learning. It is impossible to conduct a good data analysis without talking about and using machine learning. Machine learning is able to handle some of the different tasks that are needed to take all of that data we have collected and actually create some good insights and predictions out of the hidden patterns that are inside. We will also need to use machine learning, along with the help of codes that are written out in Python, to help us get started with some of our models and algorithms. These algorithms can be trained to take some or all of the data that we have available and sort through it automatically for us. This is how your business is able to go through and get those hidden insights and patterns out of the data, without having to do it manually. With this in mind, we need to take a look at some of the basics that come with machine learning. This will help us to see what machine learning is really all about, how it works, and how we are going to come to rely on it when we handle our own data analysis. The first thing that we need to take some time to explore though is the basics of machine learning. Machine learning is just going to be a method of data analysis that is able to automate some of the analytical model building that we need to deal with. It is going to be one of the branches that come with artificial intelligence and it will be based on the idea that a system is able to take data and learn from it. This system is also able to use that data to help it identify problems and make decisions. And all of this can be done with little to no intervention from humans. Because of some of the new technologies in computing that are out there, the machine learning that we are likely to see today is not going to be the same as the machine learning that may have been used in the past. Instead, it is born from pattern recognition, along with a theory that says how a computer is able to learn anything that we want,without needing to be performed to that specific task in the first place. In the beginning, researchers who were interested in some of the different parts of artificial intelligence wanted to get started by seeing if a computer or another system was able to learn from the data that we tried to present to it. The neat thing here is that machine learning is going to have an iterative aspect that will help it to learn. This is important because as the models are exposed to more and more data over time, they will be able to make the necessary adaptations along the way. What happens with machine learning is that the model is trained to adapt and to learn as needed along the way. these models are going to learn from some of the computations that happened earlier, and the hopes are that they are going to come up with some results and decisions that are repeatable and reliable. It is a science that may not be brand new, but it is gaining a lot of popularity as time goes on. While a lot of the algorithms that are available for machine learning have been around for a number of years, the ability out there to automatically apply some big and complex calculations over to the big data that we want to use, and do this in a faster method each time that we do it, is something that is more recently developed. However, even though it is recent does not mean that a lot of companies have not taken the time to learn more about it and how it is able to work for their needs. We are able to see examples of machine learning everywhere we look and as more and more businesses start to hear about data analysis, big data, and some of the other buzz words that come with machine learning, it is likely that we are going to see even more of these machine learning innovations in the future.

The Importance of Machine learning

The next thing that we need to take a look at here is why machine learning is seen as such an important thing today. There is a lot of interest out there when it comes to machine learning and all of the things that we have talked about in this guidebook, and it is definitely growing along

with things like data mining and data analysis. Things like the growing amount and types of data, the idea that we are able to process things faster and for less money, and that it is easier to store our data until we need it to have all come into play when it is time to work with machine learning.

All of these different things mean that it is very much possible for us to quickly and then automatically produce some of the models that we need. Today, and in the future, we will find that these models are able to handle and analyze ever-growing and more complex types of data while providing us with results that are very accurate and can be presented and delivered faster than ever. And the best part is that this can be done to scale, allowing us the ability to do all o this with however much data we would like.

In addition, we will find that when we are able to take the

time to build up precise models, the organization is going to have a better chance of finding opportunities that are more profitable and will put their business ahead in no time. it is even a great method to use when it is time to avoid some of the unknown risks that could face the business in the future.

Do I Really Need Machine Learning?

You may be spending some time looking through this chapter and learning a bit about machine learning, but still, feel confused as to why you would want to spend your time actually using machine learning. It may seem like something out of a book or a movie. Is it really possible to use some coding, even the basic Python code, in order to create algorithms and models that can learn? Is it actually possible for us to take our data and figure out the insights that are in it just by presenting it to a machine learning algorithm?

It may sound like something that is not reality and something from a Sci-Fi movie, but this is definitely the way that the world is taking us right now. By this, we are talking about the wide variety of entities and companies who are already jumping on board with machine learning and using it for some of their needs.

When you spend some time with machine learning, it is not going to take long before you start to see that any industry and any company, who spends time working with data and collecting it will be able to find some kind of value when they work with machine learning as well. And if you plan to do anything with data analysis, and sort through your data to figure out the best course of action to take on a regular basis, then machine learning is definitely something that you need to spend your time with overall.

With this said, there are a lot of companies in many different industries who are relying on machine learning to help them get ahead. Some of the different industries and companies who are already working with this kind of machine learning to help them out with their data analysis will include:

1.Financial services: There are so many companies within the financial sector who will be able to benefit from using machine learning to help them reach their goals. They will find that machine learning is able to help them figure out who to loan money to, how much to loan out in credit cards, who is the most likely to pay back, and how to avoid things like money laundering and fraud.

2.Healthcare: This is another industry where we are going to see a lot of big changes when it comes to how they are able to use machine learning. This is an industry that is fast paced, with very little room for error, but it is likely to see a gap in the number of people they are able to employ over the next few years. Some of the models and algorithms that we are able to create with machine learning can help to solve a few of these problems as well.

a.For example, some of the technology that is used with machine learning is already helping out these industries and providing them with a way to better serve their patients. This technology is already found in some areas like helping complete surgeries, helping to answer questions for patients, and making it easier for a doctor to complete a look over some charts and tests.

3.Oil and gas: There are also a lot of ways that this kind of industry will be able to benefit when it is time to work with machine learning. Some o these are going to include streamlining some of the distribution that the company is using in order to ensure that the process is more efficient and doesn't cost as much, learning how to predict when the sensors of the refinery are going to break, analyzing some of the minerals that are found in the ground, and finding new sources of energy to work with. The number of machine learning use cases for this kind of industry is vast and is likely to grow in the future so it is definitely something that these professionals should take a look at.

4.Government: Government agencies, including those who are in charge of utilities and other parts of public safety, may be able to find machine learning as a useful tool. They are able to take in data to figure out how to keep others as safe as possible in the long run, and it can even come into play when it is time to help the government detect fraud and minimize the amount of identity theft that is happening.

5.Retail: This is one of those industries where it may seem like machine learning is not going to matter, but when we stop and think about all of the information and data that these companies are able to gather and store about their customers, it is no wonder that they want to get in on some of the work with data analysis and machine learning as well. These retail stores are able to use this information to help them market to their customers better, provide a better recommendation system, pick out which products to sell, and more.

6.Transportation: And finally, we need to take some time to look at how the transportation industry is going to be able to use machine learning. A good way to look at this is that this industry is going to analyze data to help identify some of the trends and patterns that are found inside. This is able to help us make our routes more efficient and can be good for predicting the potential problems to increase the amount of efficiency that is found in the company.

As we can see, there are already a lot of industries and companies who have seen the value that machine learning is able to provide, and who have decided to jump on board and see how this is able to benefit them as well. Whether you are still considering adding some machine learning to your big data and seeing what insights are in that data or not, you can definitely benefit when it comes to implementing some machine learning in as well.

Machine Learning Methods

While we are here, we need to take a bit of time to look at some of the different types of machine learning algorithms. Each of these is going to be important because they are able to handle a different type of problem that we would like to handle in our algorithms and with our data. We are going to be able to bring up each one based on what we are trying to do with the data at hand.

Supervised machine learning.

This is a basic type of machine learning technique where we are going to present the algorithm with the input, and its known output at the same time. This is a good method to use because it ensures that the algorithm is able to learn based on the examples that are present.

We can think of this one like what happens when a teacher

is trying to show a new topic to their class. They are not just going to list out a few sentences about it and then expect that the students are going to know what they should do or what the right and wrong answers are. Instead, the teacher will then present some information to the students, and some examples that go along with it so that they can actually learn. This is similar to what we are going to do with supervised machine learning. This is set up to help us to work with an algorithm that is able to learn based on the input and output that we are able to provide to it. This takes some more time but can speed up the learning process because the algorithm knows exactly what examples are going to be the most useful here. A good example of this is if a bank would like to teach the algorithm of how to respond and notice fraudulent charges. The data scientist would feed in a lot of examples of past fraudulent activity so that the algorithm is able to learn about it along the way.

Unsupervised machine learning.

This one is going to be a little bit different than what we were talking about with the two other options above, mainly because it is going to not use historical labels and it is not going to be given all of the examples that we did with supervised machine learning. The system is not going to be given the right answer from the programmer when it is being set up.

The algorithm with this one needs to figure out what is being shown, all on its own. The goal with it is that we want the algorithm to explore the data and then figure out what the hidden pattern or structure is within this. Unsupervised learning is going to work the best on transactional data so that is the place where we are going to see it the most.

For example, this kind of learning is going to be able to take a look at some of the customers we are working with and then identify the segments of those customers who have similar attributes. We are then able to treat these customers the same when we work on a marketing campaign. There are a lot of great machine learning algorithms that we are able to use that fit into this, and learning how to make these works, and picking out an algorithm that fits with unsupervised machine learning can be a useful part of your data analysis.

Reinforcement learning

This is going to be the final type of machine learning that we are able to work with. This one, to those who have not spent a lot of time learning about machine learning and what it is about, may assume that unsupervised learning and reinforcement learning are the same things. And from the outside, they do appear to be similar. But we are going to spend some time looking at the differences and why reinforcement learning is going to be considered a little bit different. When we are talking about reinforcement learning, there are going to be a few things that come to mind including gamin, robotics, and navigation. With reinforcement kind of learning, the algorithm is going to be in charge of discovering, through a process of trial and error, which actions are going to provide it with some of the best rewards in the process.

Chapter 7: Python data science libraries and general libraries

Python is one of the best coding languages out there and can really help us to make use of machine learning and other algorithms that finish up our analysis. And when we combine it with some of the best data science libraries that are out there, we will find that there is so much that we can do with the data we collect. With that in mind, it is time to take a look at some of the best Python data science and data analysis libraries that can help us get our work done.

NumPy

The first library that we are going to take a look at is known as NumPy. This is going to be one of the principal packages that come with the ability to work on scientific applications. There are a lot of improvements that have been seen in this kind of library.

SciPy

Another one of the core libraries that are used in scientific computing with Python is known as SciPy. This one is going to be based on a lot of the parts of NumPy so it is often best to download both of these at the same time to utilize them well. SciPy is basically going to be a library that is able to extend the capabilities of NumPy and all that it can do.

Pandas

If you would like to do some of the more complex tasks that are found in data science and machine learning with Python, then the Pandas library is definitely a choice that you need to make. This library is able to handle all of the different parts of data science, and it is going to include algorithms to get it all done for you. There are some drawbacks that can come with it sometimes, but overall, Pandas is the one that you need.

Pandas are going to be the library that comes with Python that can provide us with some higher-level data structures, and a lot of tools that help out with the analysis.

There have actually been a few releases that are rather new with the Pandas library, and there are a ton of new features that come with it, along with bug fixes, enhancements, and API changes. The improvements are going to help out the ability that pandas has for grouping and sorting data, providing us with a more suitable output for the apply method, and some support in working on the custom operations that are needed.

Matplotlib

The next library that we need to spend some time looking at is known as Matplotlib. This is a great library to bring out when it is time to work with visualizing the data that we have and making more sense out of the other steps we have spent time on. Often visualization is one of the best things that you can work on when it comes to your work, because it helps us to make more sense out of the various complex relationships that are found in our data, so taking some time to use it and add it to your system, and getting it set up to work with Python, can be a great option. Matplotlib is going to be considered a low-level library that can work on 2D graphs and diagrams of your data. In addition, many of the other popular plotting libraries that are out there and can work with data science and data analysis are going to work along with this library, so it is one that we should spend some time with.

Of course, as this library has been around for some time, we can see that there are a lot of style changes when it comes to the colors, sizes, fonts, legends, and more that are available with this library and the visuals that it can provide.

And the types of visuals that are available with this kind of library are impressive and growing all of the time.

Scikit-Learn

If you would like to add in a bit of machine learning to the mix, then the Scikit-Learn library is one of the best ones for you to consider. Machine learning is an important part of the data analysis process because it can be combined together with the Python language to form the necessary models and algorithms to analyze your data. There are a lot of times when we need to bring some machine learning into the mix, and this library is a great option to help with it.

This is a Python library that is going to be based on the NumPy and SciPy libraries that we talked about before, so it is worth our time to download both of those and make sure they are ready to go if we want to implement some of the machine learning in this library. It is also one of the best libraries from Python that is able to work with data and get things organized and analyzed the way that we would like.

The cross-validation has been modified quite a bit, which is going to provide us with the ability to work with more than one metric at a time.

There are also a few other training methods, including the logistic regression and nearest neighbors, that have seen some great improvements over time as well.

TensorFlow

It is possible that you will want to spend some time working with deep learning and other similar methods when it comes to data analysis, and if this is your goal, then adding in the TensorFlow library is the best option to help you get this done. TensorFlow is going to be one of the popular frameworks that you can deal with when it comes to machine learning and deep learning. It was also a library that the Google Brain

Team created, so we know there are a lot of features and more that come with this library and that we can make use of as well. TensorFlow is going to provide us with a lot of abilities to work with artificial neural networks when we have more than one data set. Among the most popular, TensorFlow applications are going to include things like speech recognition and object identification to name a few.

There are going to be a few different layer helpers that work on top of regular TensorFlow that can make it easier to work with. This library is going to be quick in some of the new releases, introducing a lot of new features along the way.

Among some of the latest is going to be fixed in some of the vulnerabilities for the security of this library, and more improved integration between GPU and TensorFlow to make things easier.

PyTorch

The next library that we can talk about when it comes to working with data science. PyTorch is going to be a large framework that will allow you to get some of the computations of the tensor to perform with the GPU acceleration, create some computational graphs that are dynamic, and automatically calculate the gradients. Above this, PyTorch is going to offer us a really rich API for solving applications that are related back to neural networks.

Keras

The final Python library that works well for data science is going to be the Keras library. This one is going to be another high-level library that can help us work with neural networks, and will run on top of some of the other libraries that are out there including Theano, TensorFlow and a few other new releases. It is also possible to work the MxNet and CNTK as the backend that will be important here. It is going to be useful when you want to handle a lot of specific tasks and can reduce the amount of monotonous code that you will need to write. However, some of the more complicated types of coding that you will write out will not work as well with this option. Working with the Python library can be a great way to finish up a bunch of the tasks that you would like, and will ensure the algorithm that you work within the data science process will be done the way that you would like. Take a look at a few of these libraries and see which one is likely to provide you with some of the results that you need to get the job done.

Chapter 8: Python machine learning and data science

You may also start to notice that there are many different companies, from startups to more established firms, that are working with machine learning because they love what it is able to do to help their business grow. There are so many options when it comes to working with machine learning, but some of the ones that you may use the most often are going to include:

Statistical research:

• machine learning is a big part of IT now. You will find that machine learning will help you to go through a lot of complexity when looking through large data patterns. Some of the options that will use statistical research include search engines, credit cards, and filtering spam messages.

• Big data analysis: many companies need to be able to get through a lot of data in a short amount of time. They use this data to recognize how their customers spend money and even to make decisions and predictions about the future.

- Finances: some finance companies have also used machine learning. Stock trading online has seen a rise in the use of machine learning to help make efficient and safe decisions and so much more. As we have mentioned above, these are just three of the ways that you are able to apply the principles of machine learning in order to get the results that you want to aid in your business or even to help you create a brand new program that works the way that you want. As technology begins to progress, even more, you will find that new applications and ideas for how this should work are going to grow as well.

What is Machine Learning?

Now that we know a bit about data science, it is time to work a bit more with the specifics of machine learning. When it comes to looking at technology, you will find that machine learning is something that is really growing like crazy. You may not have been able to learn much about machine learning in the past, but it is likely that, even if you haven't done much in the world of technology, you have used machine learning in some form or another.

For example, you have probably used this kind of technology when you are using some kind of search engine to look up something online. Machine learning is the best option for you to use to make sure that you are able to make these search engines work for you. The program for the search engine is going to use machine learning to help the user get the search results that they need. And if it is set up in the right way, it is going to learn a bit from the choices of the user, helping it to become more accurate over time.

This is just one of the examples that you are able to see when it comes to technologies that will rely on machine learning. You will find that in addition to working on a search engine, including Google, this technology is going to work with some spam messages and some other applications. Unlike some of the traditional programs that you may have learned how to work within the past, machine learning is going to be able to make adjustments and changes based on the behavior of the user. This helps you to have more options and versatility about the programs that you create.

The Basics of Machine Learning

Now that we have had some time to go over a few of the basics that come with machine learning, it is time to delve in a bit more and learn how this process works, and why it is so important when you are trying to work on programs that are able to do what you want. When you are working with this kind of programming, you get the benefit of teaching a computer, or even a specific program, how to work with the experiences it has had in the past so that it can perform the way that it should in the future.

A good idea of how to illustrate this in the field is the idea of filtering out spam email. There are a few different methods that a programmer is able to use to make this one work.

While this is a memorization method that is easy to program, there are still a few things that could fail with it, and make it not work the way that you want. First, you are going to miss out on a bit of inductive reasoning in that program, which is something that must be present for efficient learning. Since you are the programmer, you will find that it is much better to go through and program the computer so that it can learn how to discern the message types that come in and that are spam, rather than trying to get the program to memorize the information.

To make sure that this process of machine learning is easy as possible, your goal would be to program the computer in a way that it is able to scan through any email that comes through the spam folder or any that it has learned is spam over time. From this scan, the program is going to be able to recognize different words and phrases that seem to be common in a message that is spam. The program could then scan through any of the newer emails that you get and have a better chance at matching up which ones should go to your inbox and which ones are spams.

You may find that this method is going to be a bit harder to program and take a bit more time, but it is a much better method to work with. You do need to take the proper precautions ahead of time with it to ensure that when the program gets things wrong (and it will make mistakes on occasion), you are able to go through and fix it fast.

There are many times that a person would be able to take a look at an email and with a glance figure out if it is spam or not. The machine learning program is going to do a pretty good job with this, but it is not perfect. You want to make sure that you are teaching it the right way to look at the emails that you get. And, sometimes, it will send perfectly good emails to the spam folder. But the more practice it gets with this and the more it learns how to work with what is spam and what isn't, the better it is going to get at this whole process.

Are there any benefits that come with machine learning?

There are a lot of different programming options that you are able to work with when it comes to making a program or doing some code. Machine learning is just one of the options that you can work with. With that said, you may be curious as to what are the benefits of working in machine learning rather than one of the other options.

At this point, you are curious as to why machine learning is going to be so great, and why you would want to make sure this is the method that you will use. There are a lot of options that you can program and code when you are working with machine learning, but we are going to focus on two main ones that are sure to make your programming needs a bit better.

The first concept that we are going to look at is the fact that machine learning means that you are able to handle any kind of task that seems too complex for a programmer to place into the computer. The second one is the idea that you are able to use the things that you learn from machine learning in order to adaptively generate all of the different tasks that you need to do. With these two concepts in mind, let's take a look at some situations where you may want to work with machine learning, where other codes and programming tricks and techniques are just not going to cut it.

Some More Complicated Tasks

The first category that we are going to look at when it comes to using machine learning is with some of the more complicated tasks that come up. There are going to be a few tasks that you are able to work on with your programming skills that, no matter how hard you try, just seem to not mesh together with traditional coding skills. These tasks may not be able to provide a high level of clarity that traditional coding need, or they have too much in terms of complexity that comes with them.

You will find that the first category of tasks that we are going to look at here is going to be any that a person or some kind of animal would be able to perform. For example, speech recognition, driving, and even image recognition would fit into here. Humans are able to do this without even thinking, but they would be really hard to teach a program to work with, especially if you are trying to use some conventional coding techniques. But machine learning will be able to step in and make sure that this works out the way that you would like.

The next issue that you may run into when working with the idea of machine learning is that it is going to handle some tasks and concepts that a human could run into some trouble. This may include doing things like going through huge amounts of data or at least a complex type of data. There are many companies who collect

114

data about their customers to use in the future. But if the company is big, that is a ton of data to work with.

While a person would be able to do this and maybe come up with a decent analysis, it would take forever. And by the time they got all of that data sorted through, there would probably be new data that needs some attention, and they would fall behind and be using outdated information. With machine learning, the business would be able to go through this information quickly and come up with some smart predictions that would be easy to use and promote the business forward.

You may find that you can use some of the concepts that come with machine learning to help with projects that work with genomic data, weather prediction, and search engines. There is going to be a lot of information that is seen as valuable with all of the different sets of data, but it is hard to find the time and the energy to go through this information. And it may not be done in a manner that is timely. But machine learning can step in and get it done.

If you have already spent some time learning about traditional programming and you know how to use a traditional coding language, then it is likely that you already know some of the cool things that you are able to do with them. But there are a lot of different things and things that will be more useful as technology progresses even more that machine learning will be able to help you to do.

Adaptively Generated Tasks

You will find that conventional programs can do a lot of really cool things, but there are some limitations to watch out for. One of these limitations is that these conventional programs are a little bit rigid. Once you write out the code and implement it, the codes are going to stay the same all the time. These codes will do the same thing over and over unless the programmer changes the code, but they can't learn and adapt.

There will be times when you are working on a program that you want to act in a different manner or react to an input that it receives. Working with a conventional program will not allow this to happen. But working with machine learning allows you to work with a method that teaches the program how to change. Spam detection in your email showed a good example of how this can work.

Machine learning is easier to work with than you would think.

Yes, there are going to be some algorithms and other tasks that come with machine learning that are more complex and take some time to learn. There are a lot of examples of what is possible with machine learning that is actually pretty simple. Your projects are going to be more complicated compared to what you saw with regular programming, but machine learning is able to take those complicated tasks and make them easier. You will be surprised at how easy it is to use the programming techniques of machine learning to do some tasks like facial recognition and speech recognition.

Machine learning is often the choice to work with because it has the unique ability to learn as it goes along the process. For example, we are able to see how this works with speech recognition. Have you ever used your smartphone or another device to talk to it and had some trouble with it being able to understand you, especially in the beginning? Over time, though, the more that you were able to use the program, the better it got at being able to understand you. In the beginning, you may have had to repeat yourself over and over again, but in the end, you are able to use it any way that you would like and it will understand you. This is an example of how machine learning is able to learn your speech patterns and understand what you are saying over time.

While machine learning is going to be able to work with a lot of different actions that may be considered complex, you will find that it is really easy to work with some of the codes that go with it and you may be surprised at how a little coding can go a long way. If you have already worked with a bit of coding and programming in the past, then you will be able to catch on quick, and it won't take much longer for those who are brand new to the idea either.

What are some of the ways that I can apply machine learning?

Now that we know a bit more about the different benefits that come with machine learning, it is time to move on and learn a bit more about some of the other things that you are going to be able to do with this as well. As you start to work with the process of machine learning a bit more, you will find that there are a lot of different ways that you are able to use it and many programmers are taking it to the next level to create things that are unique and quite fun.

You may also start to notice that there are many different companies, from startups to more established firms, that are working with machine learning because they love what it is able to do to help their business grow. There are so many options when it comes to working with machine learning, but some of the ones that you may use the most often are going to include:

• Statistical research: machine learning is a big part of IT now. You will find that machine learning will help you to go through a lot of complexity when looking through large data patterns. Some of the options that will use statistical research include search engines, credit cards, and filtering spam messages.

• Big data analysis: many companies need to be able to get through a lot of data in a short amount of time. They use this data to recognize how their customers spend money and even to make decisions and predictions about the future.

As we have mentioned above, these are just three of the ways that you are able to apply the principles of machine learning in order to get the results that you want to aid in your business or even to help you create a brand new program that works the way that you want. As technology begins to progress, even more, you will find that new applications and ideas for how this should work are going to grow as well.

Are there certain programs I can use machine learning with?

By now, you shouldn't be too surprised that there are a lot of different programs that you are able to utilize with machine learning, and many more are likely to be developed as time goes on. This makes it a really fun thing to learn how to work with and your options are pretty much going to be limited only by your imagination and coding skills.

There are a lot of different applications where you are able to use machine learning, and you will find that each of them can show you a different way that machine learning is going to work. Some examples of what you are able to do when you start to bring out machine learning will include:

- Search engines: A really good example of machine learning is with search engines. A search engine is going to be able to learn from the results that you push when you do a search. The first few times, it may not be as accurate because there are so many options, and you may end up picking an option that is further down the page. But as you do more searches, the program will learn what your preferences are and it can get better at presenting you with the choices that you want.

- Collaborative filtering: This is a challenge that a lot of online retailers can run into because they will use it to help them get more profits through sales. Think about when you are on a site like Amazon.com. After you do a few searches, you will then get recommendations for other products that you may want to try out. Amazon.com uses machine learning in order to figure out what items you would actually be interested in, in the hopes of helping you to make another purchase.

- Automatic translation: If you are working with a program that needs to translate things, then you are working with machine learning. The program needs to be able to look at a document and then recognize and understand the words that are there along with the syntax, grammar, and context of the words that are there. And then, if there are mistakes in the original document, this can make it harder for the program to learn along the way. The process of machine learning needs to teach the program how to translate a language from one point to another, and if it is able to do this with more than two languages, then it needs to learn all the different rules of grammar between each one. The programs that are out right now for this are still in beginner stages, so it's important that machine learning is used to improve them.

- Name recognition: Another option that you are able to use with machine learning is the idea of name identity recognition. This is when the program is set up so that it will recognize different entities including places, actions, and names when it is reading through a document. You will be able to work with a program and ask it to digest and then comprehend the information that it reads. This helps to find the information that is in the document much faster than you have to read through it all.

- Speech recognition: We talked about this one a bit before. But you will find that speech recognition is a great example of how you are able to work with machine learning. Speech recognition is going to be a hard thing to work with. There are so many speech patterns, differences between ages and genders, and even languages and dialects that it is hard to make any kind of program that will do well with recognizing the speech patterns of those who talk to it. But since machine learning can learn as it goes through the process, you get the benefit of having it get more familiar with your way of talking. There are going to be some mistakes and issues along the way. But if you are able to work with it and get through those early stages, the program will be able to learn and you get the benefit of getting a program that understands your requests.

- Facial recognition: And the final thing that we are going to take a look at is the idea of facial recognition. This is where the program is going to be able to look at the face of a person and recognize who they are. Or at least it will be able to tell If that person has security clearance to be in a certain area, for example. It is going to go through a series of learning processes in order to tell who is able to be on the system and who should be turned away in the process.

- There are so many cool things that you are able to do when you start to bring in some machine learning. And while all of these sound hard and would be nearly impossible with the conventional forms of programming, you will find that they can be easy and a lot of fun to work with when you are doing machine learning.

Chapter 9: The importance of data visualization

Importance of Data Visualization

There are a lot of reasons that companies are going to work with these data visuals to handle some of their workloads, and the first one is that these can help them to make better decisions. Today, more than ever, companies are relying on various data tools, including data visuals, in order to ask better questions to start with, and then make some good decisions along the way.

With the help of some of the newer computer technologies and software programs that are more user-friendly, it is easier for us to learn more about our own company and make decisions that are going to help our business while being driven by data.

The strong emphasis on some of the metrics of performance, the data dashboards, and even the KIPs, can show us all of the importance that comes with measuring and monitoring the data of the company. And when we are able to sort through all of this data and turn it into a form that we can really understand through the

graphs and charts, it becomes so much easier for us to really make the decisions that our business needs.

Another benefit is that the visuals are going to work as a way to tell meaningful stories. These graphics and visuals are going to be so important when we look at places like the mainstream media today. For example, data journalism is on the rise, and these professionals are often going to rely on some good visual tools to make it easier to tell their stories about the work that is going on around us. This can make it easier for viewers, who are just watching this information, to understand what is going on in different parts of the world.

We will also find that marketers are able to benefit from some of this, as well. Good marketers are able to make decisions that are driven by data on a daily basis, but then they need to make sure

that when they share this kind of information with their customers, they are going with a more user-friendly approach rather than just showing a bunch of data.

With the help of these visuals, the marketer is able to make all of that happen.

Being able to go through and understand, as well as read through these visuals is something that has become a requirement for those who wish to have a professional career in our modern world. Because these tools and resources are available almost everywhere, it is important, and easy to learn how to use them for some of our own needs. This is definitely something that you need to learn how to do if you wish to gain some professional careers in our modern world.

As we can see here, there are a lot of benefits that are going to come when using the data visuals for your business. And there are a lot of choices that you are able to make when it is time to bring some of these visuals out and use them for your own needs. Spending the necessary time on these, and ensuring that you have the right visual for the job at hand, and for the data that you are working with, is going to be so critical to the success that you are able to see overall.

Make sure that you take some care with the data visuals that you want to work with.

Choosing the right one and matching it up with some of the work that you are going to do along the way can make or break your project. Think about the method that will make understanding the data as easy as possible, and you will find that you can make all of this work for your needs in no time.

how data visualizations are used

These visuals are going to help us to really see what is going on, at a glance, compared to trying to read through all of the information and hoping that it is going to make sense.

For most people, we will find that working with these visuals will make it easier to see what is in all of that data and how we are able to understand what is going on. Sure, we can look through the reports and spreadsheets and more and hope that we are able to find the information that we need, but this does not always work in our favor. First off, this takes a lot more time.

When you try to look through all of that data, even after the algorithm it could be pages long, it is hard to see what is going on there, and if you do not have the right technical knowledge that comes with these algorithms, then it can get frustrating. These visuals are going to be important because they will ensure that we are able to take some of the complex relationships that are found in the data and shows them to us in just a few moments instead of having to pour over all of those documents. This doesn't mean that the documents don't have some use in our work either. It simply means that we need to take the right precautions to add in the visuals because they can definitely make the work easier.

Data visualization is basically going to be the presentation of our quantitative information in a form that is graphical. This means that we are able to use these visualizations in order to turn small and large sets of data into visuals that are going to be easier for the human brain to process and understand.

A combination of more than one visual and bits of information to help explain what is going on will be known as an infographic. Data visualizations are going to be used in order to help us to discover some of the unknown trends and facts that are found in the data that we are working with. We could see them in a lot of different forms, though, depending on the kind of information that we are trying to learn from.

They could be in the form of a line chart that is going to display some change over time. We may see them as bar and column charts that can help us to make some comparisons and observe relationships. And pie charts are going to be able to showcase parts of a whole that we want to keep track of.

Chapter 10: The Data Science pipeline

Binary classification; PCA; PCA for Data Visualization; PCA to Speed-up Machine Learning algorithms; the covariance of the Matrix.

We will be looking at one of the most common classification algorithms – decision trees. Decision trees are one of the most ubiquitous and powerful classification algorithms available. This algorithm can be used for both continuous as well as categorical output variables. As we know classification algorithms are that category of algorithms used to predict the category of the given input data.

The objective is to create a model that predicts the value of a target based on simple decision rules that are inferred from the data features.

In simple words, it is very similar to the common -if.. then.. else.. conditional statement that is commonly used as part of programming languages. This is more like a flow chart and is like a branch based decision system. This algorithm is something that even a very average person can understand - something like looking at an incoming email and classifying it as personal or work or spam email based on certain pre defined rules can be given as a very simple use case of decision trees.

A decision tree is literally a tree where one can take the route of either of the branches based on the answer to the conditional question at each node, each branch represents a possible course action. Below is a simple decision tree example from real life, where the tree can be used to determine if a person is fit or not

Image: A simple illustration of a Decision tree.

Advantages Of Decision Trees

Some key advantages of using decision trees are

133

Simple to understand and interpret and easy to visualize

This model requires little to no data preparation while other techniques require various steps such normalizing the input data set, dummy variables to be created, blank or null values have to be cleaned up and various such scrubbing and reducing activity which are normally done are not required. This significantly reduced the time and cost of execution of using this machine learning model. It is however important to remember, this model will require missing data to be filled up, else will thrown an error and not proceed with further computation.

The number of data points determines the cost of execution. The relationship of cost to number of data is logarithmic to train the data model.

The other unique strength of this data model is it works well with both numerical as well as categorical data while several other techniques are usually specially designed to work with one format of the data or the other.

Ability to handle multi output problems

It used the white box mode that is if a given solution is observable in a model, the explanation for the condition can be easily explained using a Boolean logic equation. Whereas in case of algorithms based on black box model – like a synthetic neural network and the outcome could be tough to understand.

The other advantage is the ability to evaluate the model by using statistical trials, thus making the model more reliable that the others.

This model also performs well if the assumption on data sets is slightly violated when applying to the actual model, thus ensuring flexibility and accurate results irrespective of variance.

Disadvantages Of Decision Trees

This can be overcome using techniques like pruning (literally like pruning the branch of tree, but is currently not supported in python libraries) - the task is to set up few samples needed at a leaf node or setting the highest depth a tree can grow to, thus limiting the problem of overfitting.

The trees become unstable because of small variations in the input data, resulting in an entirely different tree getting generated. This issue can be overcome by using a decision tree within an ensemble.

NP-Complete problem - a very common theoretical computer science problem can be a hindrance in the attempt to design the most optimal decision tree, because under several aspects, the optimality can become affected. As a result, heuristic algorithms such as greedy algorithms where local optimal decisions at each node may become an issue. Teaching multiple trees to a collaborative learner can again reduce the effect of this issue and the feature and samples can be randomly sampled with replacements.

Concepts such as XOR, parity or multiplexer issues can be difficult to compute and express with decision trees.

In case of domination of classes, the tree learners end up creating biased learners. It is therefore important to balance the data set prior to fitting with the decision tree.

It is important to be conscious of the factor that decision trees tend to over fit the data with a large number of features and getting the right sample to number the features has to be taken care to not become too highly dimensional.

Decision tree is extensively used in designing intelligent home automation systems - say, if the current temperature, humidity and other factors are at a certain level, then control the home cooling system temperature accordingly type systems are largely designed based on decision trees. Things like an average human deciding to go out and play a game of gold can be a series of decisions and can be modeled around a decision tree.

There are two key factors

Entropy - measure of randomness or impurity of the sample set - this must be low!

Information Gain - also called as entropy reduction is the measure of how much the entropy has changed after splitting the dataset - the value of this must be high.

In statistical modeling, you might notice that reversion analysis aims to be a process which helps estimate the various relationships between different variables. This will include several techniques that are typically used for variable analysis and matching when several variables are worked with at once whenever you are showing the relationship between independent and dependent variables.

Reversion analysis is a valuable tool when it comes to understanding how the usual value for variable changes over time. Reversion will also help you estimate the conditional expectation of a variable that depends on the independent variable and the average value of said variable. Briefly put, it will shorten the time you spend while juggling multiple values.

More uncommon are situations where you will be presented with a variable that depends on the independent variable along with its quantile or location parameters for the conditional distribution. Usually, the estimate you come to will be an expression for the

138

independent value. We call this the reversion expression. In reversion analysis, you will be showing your interest in the characterization of the variation of the dependent variable in relation to the expression which we can describe as the probability distribution.

One of the possible approaches is taking a conditional analysis. This will take the estimate for the maximum over the average for the dependent variables, which are, again, based on the independent variable that is given. This allows you to determine if the independent variable is necessary or sufficient for the value that the dependent variable holds.

You will use reversion when you are looking to forecast and when it overlaps with machine learning. It will be a good tool for when you are trying the relationships between dependent and independent variables. When dealing with a restricted circumstance, reversion will be used to infer the causal relationship between the variables. You should be cautious, however, as it may give you a false relationship.

There are several different techniques for reversion. Linear reversion and least squares diversion are two of them. Your reversion expression will be defined as finite numbers which don't have a parameter. Nonparametric reversion is a tool that we will be utilizing when we want to permit the reversion expression to be used as a collection of expressions for infinite dimensionality.

Your performance when it comes to revision analysis is going to be a summary of the methods that you practice as processes for data generation and how it ties back into the reversion approach that you applied. The true form of data generation is not always going to be known as reversion analysis and depends on the extent of your assumptions.

The assumptions you provide will need to be testable so you can see if you have provided the machine with enough data.

Machine Learning and Robotics

I believe that we have helped you grow more familiar with what machine learning is. It should not surprise you that it sparked an interest in robotics and has stayed roughly the same for the past several years. But are robots related to machine learning?

Robotics has not developed too much in the past several years. However, these developments are a great foundation for discoveries to come and some even relate to machine learning.

When it comes to robotics, the following five applications apply in machine learning:

1. **Computer vision:** some would say that robot vision and machine vision are more correct as far as terminology goes. For a very long time, engineers and roboticists have been trying to develop a type of camera that will let a robot process the physical world around him as data. Robot vision and machine vision are two terms that go hand in hand. Their creation can be credited to the existence of automated inspection systems and robot guidance. The two have a very small difference and it comes in regards to kinematics in the use of robot vision. It encompasses the calibration of the comment frame and enhances the robot's ability to affect its surroundings physically.

The already impressive advances in computer vision that have been instrumental in coming up with techniques that are geared for prediction learning, has been further helped by a huge influx of data.

2. **Imitation learning:** this is relatively closely connected to observational learning. It is common with kids and has common features, the most obvious being probabilistic models and Batesian. The main question, however, stands. Will it find use in humanoid robots?

Imitation learning has always been an important part of robotics as it has features of mobility that transcend those of factory settings in domains like search and rescue construction, which makes the programming robotic solutions manually a puzzle.

3. **Self-Supervised learning:** Allows robots to generate their training instance due to the self-supervised learning approaches, in order to improve their performance. This includes priority training, as well as data that is captured and is used to translate vague sensor data. The robots with optical devices that have this installed can reject and detect objects.

A solid example called Watch-Bot has been created by Cornell and Stanford. It utilized a laptop and laser pointer, a 3D sensor, and a camera in order to find normal human activities like patterns that are learned through the methods of probability. A laser pointer is used to detect the distance to the object. Humans are notified 60 percent of the time, as the robot has no concept of what he is doing and why he is doing it.

4. **Medical and assistive technologies:** A device that senses and oversees the processing of sensory information before setting an action that is going to benefit a senior or someone with incapacities. This is the basic definition of the assistive robot. They have a capacity for movement therapy, as well as the ability to provide other therapeutic and diagnostic benefits. They are quite cost-prohibitive for hospitals in the US and abroad, so they still haven't left the lab.

Robotics in the field of medicine has advanced at a rapid rate even though they are not used by medical facilities. This advancement can be seen clearly if you see the capabilities of these robots.

5. **Multi-Agent learning:** It offers some key components such as negotiation and coordination. This involves that the robot, based on machine learning,

finds equilibrium strategies and adapts to a shifting landscape.

During late 2014, an excellent example of an algorithm used by distributed robots or agents was made in one of MIT's labs for decision and information systems. The robots collaborated and opted to build a more inclusive and better learning model than that which was done by a single robot. They did so via building exploration and teaching them to find the quickest ways through the rooms in order to construct a knowledge base in an autonomous manner.

Python and machine learning

Have you been using the classification as a type of machine learning? Probably yes, even if you did not know about it. Example: The email system has the ability to automatically detect spam. This means that the system will analyze all incoming messages and mark them as spam or non-spam.

Often, you, as an end user, have the option to manually tag messages as spam, to improve the ability to detect spam. This is a form of machine learning where the system takes the examples of two types of messages: spam and so-called ham (the typical term for "non-spam email") and using these cases automatically classify incoming mails fetched.

What is a classification? Using the examples from the same domain of the problem belonging to the different classes of the model train or the "generate rules" which can be applied to (previously unknown) examples.

Dataset Iris is a classic collection of data from the 1930s; This is one of the first examples of modern statistical classifications. These measurements allow us to identify the different types of flower.

Today, the species are identified through DNA, but in the 30s the role of DNA in genetics had not yet been recorded. Four characteristics were selected for each plant sepal length (length of cup slip) sepal width (width of cup slip) petal length, and petal width. There are three classes that identify the plant: Iris setosa, Iris versicolor, and Iris virginica.

Formulation of the problem

This dataset has four characteristics. In addition, each plant species was recorded, as well as the value of class characteristics. The problem we want to solve is: Given these examples, can we anticipate a new type of flower in the field based on measurements?

This is the problem of classification or supervised learning, where based on the selected data, we can "generate rules" that can later be applied to other cases. Examples for readers who do not study botany are: filtering unwanted email, intrusion detection in computer systems and networks, detection of fraud with credit cards, etc.

Data Visualization will present a kind of triangle, circle type, and virginica type of mark x.

The model has already discussed a simple model that achieves 94% accuracy on the entire data set. The data we use to define what would be the threshold was then used to estimate the model.

What I really want to do is to assess the ability of generalization model. In other words, we should measure the performance of the algorithm in cases where classified information, which is not trained, is used.

Transmitting device stringent evaluation and use the "delayed" (Casually, Held-out) data is one way to do this.

However, the accuracy of the test data is lower! While this may surprise an inexperienced person who is engaged in machine learning, it's expected to be lower by veterans. Generally, the accuracy of testing is lower than the accuracy of training. Using the previous examples you should be able to plot a graph of this data. The graph will show the boundary decisions.

Consider what would happen if the decision to limit some of the cases near the border were not there during the training? It is easy to conclude that the boundaries move slightly to the right or left.

NOTES: In this case, the difference between the accuracy of the measured data for training and testing is not great. When using a complex model, it is possible to get 100% accuracy in training and very low accuracy testing! In other words, the accuracy of the training set is a too optimistic assessment of how good your algorithm is. Experiments always measured and reported the accuracy of testing and accuracy on the set of examples that are not being used for the training!

A possible problem with the hold-out validation is that we are only using half of the data used for training. However, if you use too much data for training, assessment error testing is done on a very small number of examples. Ideally, we would use all the data for the training and all the data for testing, but it was impossible.

A good approximation of the impossible ideals is a method called cross-validation. The simplest form of cross-validation is Leave-one-out cross-validation.

When using cross-checking, each example was tested on a model trained without taking into account that data. Therefore, cross-validation is a reliable estimate of the possibilities of generalization model. The main problem with the previous method of validation is a need for training of a large number (the number grows to the size of the set).

Instead, let's look at the so-called v-fold validation. If, for example, using 5-fold cross-validation, the data is divided into five parts, of which in each iteration 4 parts are used for training and one for testing.

The number of parts in the initial set of components depends on the size of the event, the time required for the training model, and so on. When generating fold data, it is very important to be balanced.

CONCLUSION

Data analysis plays an important role in many aspects of life today. From the moment you wake up, you interact with data at different levels. A lot of important decisions are made based on data analytics. Companies need this data to help them meet many of their goals. As the population of the world keeps growing, their customer base keeps expanding. In light of this, it is important that they find ways of keeping their customers happy while at the same time meeting their business goals.

Given the nature of competition in the business world, it is not easy to keep customers happy. Competitors keep preying on each other's customers, and those who win have another challenge ahead - how to maintain the customers lest they slide back to their former business partners. This is one area where data analysis comes in handy.

In order to understand their customers better, companies rely on data. They collect all manner of data at each point of interaction with their customers. This data is useful in several ways. The companies learn more about their customers, thereafter clustering them according to their specific needs. Through such segmentation, the company can attend to the customers' needs better, and hope to keep them satisfied for longer.

But, data analytics is not just about customers and the profit motive. It is also about governance. Governments are the biggest data consumers all over the world. They collect data about citizens, businesses, and every other entity that they interact with at any given point. This is important information because it helps in a lot of instances.

For planning purposes, governments need accurate data on their population so that funds can be allocated accordingly. Equitable distribution of resources is something that cannot be achieved without proper data analysis. Other than planning, there is also the security angle. To protect the country, the government must maintain different databases for different reasons. You have high profile individuals who must be accorded special security detail, top threats who must be monitored at all times, and so forth. To meet the security objective, the government has to obtain and maintain updated data on the persons of interest at all times.

There is so much more to data analysis than the corporate and government decisions. As a programmer, you are venturing into an industry that is challenging and exciting at the same time. Data doesn't lie, unless of course it is manipulated to, in which case you need insane data analysis and handling skills. As a data analyst, you will come across many challenges and problems that need solutions which can only be handled through data analysis. The way you interact with data can make a big difference, bigger than you can imagine.

There are several tools you can use for data analysis. Many people use Microsoft Excel for data analysis and it works well for them. However, there are limitations of using Excel which you can overcome through Python. Learning Python is a good initiative, given that it is one of the easiest programming languages. It is a high-level programming language because its syntax is so close to the normal language we use. This makes it easier for you to master Python concepts.

For expert programmers, you have gone beyond learning about the basics of Python and graduated into using Python to solve real-world problems. There are many problems that can be solved through data analysis. The first challenge is usually understanding the issue at hand, then working on a data solution for it.

This book follows a series of elaborate books that introduced you to data analysis using Python. There are some important concepts that have been reiterated since the beginning of the series to help you remember the fundamentals. Knowledge of Python libraries is indeed important. It is by understanding these libraries that you can go on to become an expert data analyst with Python.

As you interact with data, you do understand the importance of cleaning data to ensure the outcome of your analysis is not flawed. You will learn how to go about this, and build on that to make sure your work is perfect. Another challenge that many organizations have is protecting the integrity of data. You should try and protect your organization from using contaminated data. There are procedures you can put in place to make sure that you use clean data all the time.

We live in a world where data is at the center of many things we do. Data is produced and stored in large amounts daily from automated systems. Learning data analysis through Python should help you process and extract information from data and make meaningful conclusions from them. One area where these skills will come in handy is forecasting. Through data analysis, you can create predictive models that should help your organization meet its objectives.

A good predictive model is only as good as the quality of data introduced into it, the data modeling methods, and more importantly the dataset used for the analysis. Beyond data handling and processing, one other important aspect of data analysis is visualization. Visualization is about presentation. Your data model should be good enough for an audience to read and understand it at the first point of contact. Apart from the audience, you should also learn how to plot data on different visualizations to help you get a rough idea of the nature of data you are working with.

When you are done with data analysis, you should have a data model complete with visual concepts that will help in predicting outcomes and responses before you can proceed to the testing phase. Data analysis is a study that is currently in high demand in different fields. Knowing what to do, as well as when and how to handle data, is an important skill that you should not take for granted. Through this, you can build and test a hypothesis and go on to understand systems better.